Comparing Mythologies
Tomson Highway

National Library of Canada Cataloguing in Publication

Highway, Tomson, 1951–
    Comparing mythologies / Tomson Highway; introduction by
John Moss.

(Charles R. Bronfman lecture in Canadian studies)
ISBN 0-7766-0567-4

    1. Indian mythology. 2. Christianity. 3. Mythology, Greek.
    I. Moss, John, 1940– II. Title. III. Series.

BL315.H54 2003   291.1   C2003-902405-9

Copyediting: Käthe Roth

Proofreading: Carol Tobin

Cover illustration: Luong Lê-Phan, University of Ottawa

ISBN 0-7766-0567-4

Charles R. Bronfman Lecture in Canadian Studies

Comparing Mythologies

Tomson Highway

The Opposite of Prayer:
An Introduction to Tomson Highway
by John Moss

Public Lecture
23 September 2002
University of Ottawa

University of Ottawa Press

Conférence Charles R. Bronfman en Études canadiennes

Cette conférence de prestige annuelle se tient grâce à un don de Charles R. Bronfman auquel s'ajoute une subvention d'appoint du ministère du Patrimoine canadien. Le but de la conférence est d'encourager la diffusion du savoir par l'invitation de personnalités qui ont contribué de façon significative à l'étude du Canada. Compte tenu du caractère bilingue de l'Université d'Ottawa et de sa situation au cœur de la capitale nationale, la conférence Charles R. Bronfman a lieu sur une base d'alternance dans l'une ou l'autre des langues officielles du pays.

Charles R. Bronfman Lecture in Canadian Studies

This distinguished annual lecture is made possible thanks to a donation from Charles R. Bronfman and to a grant from the Canadian Studies Program of the Department of Canadian Heritage. The lecture seeks to promote scholarship by inviting personalities who have made significant contributions to the study of Canada. Given the bilingual character of the University of Ottawa and its location in the heart of the nation's capital, the Charles R. Bronfman lecture is given in one or the other of Canada's official languages, on an alternating basis.

The Opposite of Prayer:
An Introduction to Tomson Highway

by John Moss

In an ironic conflation of mythologies, the techno-cultural, I did a web search for Tomson Highway. I came up with one thousand, nine hundred and eighty entries the first time I tried, and two thousand and twenty-four the second time, using the same search engine. I am dealing with a trickster, I thought, but was not sure whether the trickster was Google or Tomson Highway. The mean between 1980 and 2024 is 2002. It's too neat, I thought, perhaps there is a conspiracy between Highway and technology. After a great deal of consideration, I concluded this was not the case, and that each was a trickster in his or in its own way (despite Highway's mutations of gender for dramatic interrogation, I could not bring myself to give Google sex).

The most interesting line in my search read as follows, and gave me strong reason to consider the capacity for facts to obscure the truth:

> Born in 1951 in a tent on his father's
> trapline, as a small boy Mr. Highway
> discovered the piano.

I expected this to be followed by, "Living in foster homes from fifteen, Mr. Highway studied music in London, England." Or, "In attending a performance of *Les Belles Sœurs* by Michel Tremblay with James Reaney, and working on Reaney's dramatization of John Richardson's *Wacousta* in London, Ontario, Mr. Highway was nominated for the Governor General's Award. Several Times." Or, "Receiving the Chalmers and Dora Mavor Moore Awards for drama, he is Cree."

Facts are only the random detritus of our lives until they are connected by story. Stories, to paraphrase Robert Kroetsch, make us real. If there is anything like truth accessible to us in the world, it must be through the ways we tell of ourselves to each other. For such sharing, we use words, design images, make music, and dance, we make what in our world we call art, and what is elsewhere accepted as the warp in the fabric of life; the weft is the time of our hearing, or watching, or listening. Tomson Highway, through his life as a musician and social worker, writer and dramaturge, shares sometimes uncomfortable truths, sometimes beautiful truths, and sometimes truth that we know only because we feel it within, where it haunts us with tears and with laughter.

The word "beautiful" resonates. He is a beautiful writer: comic, angry, poetic, sad. His English echoes the cadences of another language— not only the images but the sounds themselves—the music of another world. He brings Cree to English the way Chinua Achebe plays out the inflections of the Ibo language and doomed Biafra into English, transforming the syntax of imperial subjugation into something new and so vital that the language itself is transformed into the voice of the people whose lives it organized nearly to extinction.

Listen to Highway, as the Fur Queen's lips "began descending. Down they came, fluttering like a leaf from an autumn birch, until they came to rest on Abraham's left cheek. There." Listen to English, itself, described as "hard, filled with sharp jagged angles;" listen, as "slowly, ever so slowly, the ghost baby tumbled, head over heels over head, down, down to earth." And listen, as the lovely Mariesis Okimasis in orgasm envisions that baby, "a sleeping child, not born yet but fully formed, naked, curled up inside the womb of night, tumbling down towards her and her husband."

As Rudy Wiebe says in his story "Where Is the Voice Coming From?" I think it is Cree that I hear, but I do not speak Cree myself. Nor Ibo. But Highway, like Achebe, shifts the walls of my English labyrinth. He opens my way as his reader to worlds

I could never have otherwise known. I have eaten raw caribou, I am a man of the world. I wear my Mowhawk ancestry on my lapel; I have no need for an Order of Canada. Like Tomson Highway, I think in trilogies. The funniest man I know, since Matt Cohen died, is my friend Drew Hayden Taylor from the Curve Lake Reserve. I admire Thomas King. I choke with laughter and fear when I listen to the words of Alootook Ipellie. It is the particularities of fiction, the absurdities, that make us real.

Tomson Highway gives us a renewed sense of place with words as familiar once read as the environs of Yoknapatawpha, which is William Faulkner's great gift to the world. I have been to Eemanapiteepitat and I did not want ever to leave and live in a residential school run by the church that would work with the state to drown with their vaulting resources my small boy's mind and body, but from which I will emerge able to breathe under-water and hear the music of stars.

Could I ask you to shut your eyes. Now, open your minds. Think of this as the opposite of prayer. With eyes closed, look down, down through the surface veneer beneath your feet, past the floor joists and structural shadows, look down until you see the earth. The building disappears, and you are a witness, but time has collapsed and you are not here. Look around you. At first you see forest, great pines and rich flora, then you see water, a riverbank, and you hear the sound of fish swimming and butterfly wings—that's how attuned you are to your surroundings, how inseparable you are from the natural world.

And only now do you see the people. You were blind to their presence because their reality is different from yours. The people around you occupy space the way you occupy time. Their existence approaches transparency. And they cannot see you, you are confined by what Blake called the limits of opacity. These people do not dwell on the land the way you are accustomed to. There are many of them, they have been here in their millions over thousands of years. When the great Sphinx of Egypt crawled out of the sands by the Nile, and

Stonehenge was rising in ominous rings from the Salisbury Plains, these people were here. Their genius, to leave no monuments; their genius, to envision the circle of creation as complete.

What do you call these people in your language? Do you use adjectives, twisted into nouns? "Natives." "Aboriginals." "Savages" no longer applies, although the word was used by cultural icons like Ernest Thompson Seton and Catherine Parr Traill for thematic effect. Perhaps you say "Indigene." A bloodless corruption. Perhaps "Indians." My dictionary has no entry for "Indian." There are compound entries for "Indian agent," "Indian corn," "Indian hemp," "Indian pipe," "Indian pony," "Indian rice," "Indian summer," and "Indian tobacco," all of which are defined in relation to the indigenous peoples of North America, where the word "Indian" has noun value. Interspersed alphabetically are entries such as "Indian English," "Indian Standard Time," "Indian Subcontinent." This "Indian" is adjectival, and refers to another hemisphere. It is as confusing as having two football teams called the Rough Riders. But the significance is lethal. There is nothing playful in the narrative concealed or exposed in the play between "Indian" as a subject or object, and "Indian" as modification. Ask the Tema-augami Anishnabi living on a small island in Lake Temagami. Ask the last of the Mahican. Ask a Cree like Tomson Highway, with degrees in music and literature, with honorary doctorates and innumerable accolades, whose father and mother worked traplines and lost so many of their children to death and a residential school in The Pas.

While searching the web I discovered that information about Tomson Highway could be found at ‹www.news.cornell.edu/chronicles/8.23.01 /Indians_India.› The ambiguity was amplified when I read that he was included in the Cornell file under the rubric, "Indians' Indians: (Re)Presentations of Native American People in the Arts." After trying to sort out whether or not "Indians'" with an apostrophe was adjectival, that is, concerning people from an Asian subcontinent possessed of Indian characteristics, or a noun, and therefore implying cultural ownership over other people, also designated Indians, I retreated to consider the absence of the word "Canada." "Native American" is confusing, somehow it is oxymoronic, it demeans or obscures the people it is meant to celebrate.

Tomson Highway is Cree, and, to use the word properly, a "native" to the land of his forebears, inseparable from the earth and its people. Tomson Highway is Canadian. These are not mutually exclusive. In fact, in his celebrated plays like *Dry Lips Oughta Move to Kapuskasing* and *The Rez Sisters*, in beautiful children's books such as *Kiweeginapiseek*, or in English *Dragonfly Kites*, in his novel *Kiss of the Fur Queen*, in his speeches and public persona, in his influence as artistic director on productions from the Native Earth Performing Arts company, he proves the absurdity of the hyphen. He is not Cree-Canadian or Canadian-Cree; he is Cree and he is Canadian. To be Cree is to originate in the land, long before it became known as a continent or was named by invaders, long before northern

Manitoba was measured by distance and direction from Greenwich in England and declared to be remote, or was measured by the culture and politics of the settler contagion and found to be dangerous and also irrelevant. To be Canadian is more elusive, intrinsic to the experience of each generation in turn. As a Cree, Tomson Highway is telling our story and I am learning to be what I am.

This is what I think he is saying. But I do not, of course, understand Cree myself.

Comparing Mythologies

Good evening, ladies and gentlemen. I am here to talk about mythology. I am here to talk about mythology because, after fifty years of living and watching—and studying—my people, my culture, my language, my land, go through the experience they have gone through since the year 1492, I have come to believe that if the well-being, or the illness, of a people and the environment they inhabit has its roots anywhere, then that's where those roots lie. I am here to talk about mythology because I believe that if the consciousness of a people has its roots anywhere, then that's where those roots lie. I am here to talk about mythology because I believe that if the language, just for instance, of a people, the very tool by which that people articulates life both inside it and life all around it, has its origins anywhere, then that's where lie those origins. I am here to talk about mythology because I believe that if the very nerve pulse of the life of a people, the electrical impulse that sparks into action the life of a people, comes from anywhere, then that's where it comes from. I am here to talk about mythology because I believe that without mythology, we would be nothing but walking corpses, zombies, mere empty hulks of animal flesh and bone, skin and blood and liquid matter with no purpose, no reason for existing, no use, no point, nothing, mere flesh and bone and skin and blood with nowhere to go, and with no guide to guide it through a life path that, one imagines, has been given to us all by . . . what? Who? Why? And why here? These are the questions mythology answers, I feel very strongly, more so than theology, just for instance.

What, however, is mythology? What is it about the "discipline" of mythology that makes it stand quite unique as a discipline amongst an

immense field of disciplines that can range anywhere from quantum physics to cellular biology to
philosophy to anthropology to sociology to psy-
chology to geography to history to theology and on
and on and on *ad infinitum?* What is it about
mythology that differentiates it, and differentiates it
utterly, from any other field of intellectual activity?

The comparisons, of course, are limitless,
but sociology, to pick one other discipline just to
start with, tells the story of human interaction, the
way people, communities, and societies interact
with one another on a day-to-day, week-to-week,
year-to-year basis, how they communicate, how
they live together or against each other. Geography,
to pick another, tells the story of a landscape; geography, that is to say, defines all the physical features
of a land from its rivers to its mountains to its val-
leys to its fields to its forests to its towns and its
cities. History tells the story of the *physical* movements of a people across that landscape. And
mythology tells the story of the *spiritual* movements
of that people across that landscape. If geography, in

other words, were like looking at the photograph of a river, say, or a mountain or a hill or a forest or a valley or a city, and if history were like looking at the photograph of the physical, exterior shape of a person, and sociology were like looking at the photograph of people in family and community groupings of one sort or another with their various modes of dress and of grooming and of tools, accoutrements, habitat and such, then mythology would be like looking at the negative of a person, an X-ray—that is to say, one, however, that outlines not the bone structure nor the internal organs of that person nor the veins nor the nerves (for these, too, are physical) but, rather, one that delineates the *spiritual* nervous system, as it were—and that system only—of that person, that tangle of electrical cords and wiring in all its wondrous, mystical, magical complexity. That, to me, is at least one definition of mythology that distinguishes it as a field of thought and of study from all others, including, most essentially, theology which I believe to be its nearest rival, so to speak, or its nearest cousin.

Mythology, of course, comes to us from the Greek word "myth," whose meaning is "narrative," or "story," and "logos," whose meaning is "word" or "discourse," while theology comes, in the same language, from "theos," meaning "god" or "divinity" and, of course, the aforementioned "logos." So that the former ends up being a discourse on narrative, or the art of story-telling, including, most notably, a narrative on all three of humankind, animalkind, *and* god, the latter a discourse on god (or gods), and god only.

Now, in the language of my people, one that I knew way before I became conversant in the English or French languages, there are three distinct terms for the concept of narrative. The first term is *achimoowin*, which means "to tell a story" or "to tell the truth." The second is *kithaskiwin*, which means "to tell a lie," meaning "to weave a web of fiction," as it were. And the third, which lies at a point exactly halfway between these first two is *achithoogeewin*, which means "to mythologize." Meaning that the visionaries of my people, the thinkers who gave birth and shape to the Cree language as we know it today, chose the exact halfway point between truth and lie, non fiction and fiction, to situate mythology. And here I'll tell you a little story that illustrates this little principle:

One night, about twenty years ago, a most unruly and rather spectacular celebration was taking place at a hotel room in downtown Toronto that I, most unfortunately, was ignorant of at the time and so failed completely to attend, rats. As with most of our parties, this one was unruly and spectacular because a clown—a laughing deity, that is to say, one called, in English, the Trickster—lives inside our language and thus inside us, about which more shortly. So wild was the party, in fact, that the police eventually came calling. The thing, you see, was that my dear friend and colleague—Billy Boy Cutthroat, we shall call him, for purposes of concealing his true identity—had been fuelling the event with the liberal supply of some magical tobacco that he always seemed to have on his person all through those years, a substance that, by the way—and I must say this here—is infinitely, infinitely more conducive to the health of Indian reserves across this country than alcohol has ever, ever been. The knock on the door, at any rate, came and someone in the room yelled "Police." At which point, my friend Billy Boy Cutthroat rushed to the window, which was open, and jumped out. From the thirtieth floor! And it was said, for many years thereafter, that he hung on to a window ledge somewhere just below that thirtieth-floor window for "hours," all while the police searched the room inside out for evidence of criminal activity of the sort for which Billy Boy Cutthroat had gained, over the years, such glamorous notoriety. That the floor was the thirtieth was the lie. That was the fiction. That was outright *kithaskiwin*.

As I wandered my way across Ontario that next year (for that's the kind of job I had at the time), as I, *par hasard*, traced this story from city to reserve to town and back to city, that thirtieth floor in that hotel room became the twenty-fifth, then the twentieth, then the fifteenth, then the tenth, etc., etc., etc. until, about a whole year later, I got to

Mr. Cutthroat himself, who, by the way, lived on a reserve way up in . . . well, somewhere in the north. At any rate, by the time I got to him, the source of the "myth," that is to say, that hotel room in Toronto, had been not on the thirtieth floor nor the twentieth nor the tenth, nor the seventh, not even the third. It had been the second! And he hadn't hung onto that window ledge for hours, he had merely dropped to the ground, suffered a few minor bruises, one sore ankle, and then sort of hobbled off down the alleyway, round the corner, and down the street to the nearest bar, which, of course, just happened to be there. That was the truth, that was the non fiction. That was *achimoowin.*

At a point exactly halfway between these two stories, or the two versions of this story, that is to say, at a point exactly halfway between the lie about this "narrative" and the truth about this "narrative," of course, lies the narrative that I heard from who was perhaps the tenth teller of the tale (and way before I caught up with my friend up north). By this tenth telling of the story, that is to say, I had it firmly implanted in my mind—in my dream world, so to speak—that plain, old, ordinary human being Billy Boy Cutthroat not only had the fingernails of Superman himself but had sprouted the wings of an angel, which, of course, is how he managed to hover Holy Spirit–like high up in the air just outside that window on what I dreamt was the ninetieth floor of some extraordinary hotel in downtown Toronto. That was the myth. That was the dream. That was *achithoogeewin*. And that, ladies and gentlemen, is precisely the region of our collective dream world, our collective subconscious, where men sprout wings, horses sprout wings, creatures half-man and half-horse once walked this Earth, that is the region of our lives where people exist who are half-man and half-goat, half-woman and half-fish, half-man and half-coyote, half-woman and half-spider, snakes talk to women (but not to men), women give birth without having had sex, men—and women, too—are half-human and half-divine. And an old man up in the sky with a great white beard can part Lake Ontario right down the middle with one wave of his hand, so we Ontarians can shop in Rochester, New York, without having first to pass through Buffalo, Gananoque, or even Pearson Airport . . . and anyone pursuing us gets drowned to his death. That's another definition of mythology that, it seems to me, makes much sense.

The last definition that I wish to give of mythology, for the purposes of this lecture—which brings us round to the first quite neatly—is that mythology defines, mythology maps out, the collective subconscious, the collective dream world of races of people, the collective spirit of races of people, the collective spiritual nervous system, if you will, where every cord, every wire, every filament has a purpose and a function, every twitch a job in the way that collective human body, mind, and soul moves and operates from one day to the next to the next and to the next. Without this *mechanism*, that is to say, there would be no reason for getting up in the morning to go to work, to school, or to play. Life would have no meaning. And suicide would flourish.

The world, however, is filled with mythology—or, rather, mythologies—as who in their right mind doesn't know. Every race, every language, even every city, every town, every village has its own. Many hold immense similarity one to the other, many differ quite drastically, but the fact remains that each and every one of these mythologies defines the collective dream world, the collective subconscious of that people; it, in other words, is the principle, or driving force, that decides whether nature or our bodies, just for instance, are friends or foes, enemies to be conquered or lovers to be loved, gardens to be killed or gardens to be tilled.

To study each mythology extant on the planet, however, would take ten lifetimes, easy, to accomplish. With this lecture, we have time for three—and this with a superficiality and cursoriness so extreme you will probably laugh at me, rise from your seats, insult me, and leave—three, in any case, that I have selected if only for the reason that these, to my way of thinking, are the three that have had most to do with the development and the shaping of the society we know today, at the turn of the century, as North American society, the three that have had most to do with the development and the shaping of this society as it thinks, this society as it lives, this society as it dreams. And these three "narratives," so to speak, are Christian mythology, Greek mythology, and North American Aboriginal mythology, specifically, in my case, Cree mythology, Cree *achithoogeewin*. I have, moreover, selected them because they offer, they teach, they promulgate three distinct ways of thinking, of relating to our planet, of relating to our universe, of relating to our bodies and ourselves, of relating to the very environment in which, and because of which, we live, breathe, and walk.

The first mythology, of course—and by "first," I mean Christian mythology—defines a collective subconscious that is structured on, is governed and guided by, the principle of one straight line. In the beginning was this void, this endless soupy mass of matter that, according to the physicist Herr Heinz Pagels, pulsated and danced and swirled through the great dome of space. From this great swirl of nothingness emerged a God who, first of all, was male, and male entirely, one, moreover, who had seemingly no need of partnership from or collaboration with a female to give birth, by himself, to the universe with its planets and its stars and its moons and the Earth with its soil and its rock and its magic molecules. That was the beginning of time, the beginning of that straight line on the first day of which, of course, this male God gave birth to light, on the second day of which he gave birth to water, etc., until, on the sixth day he created man from a little ball of mud; woman came later; she wasn't necessary, not really. And the narrative goes on from there, the most salient feature to note being that this male God gave man the power to rule over nature, to exploit it, and to do with it as he pleased. The middle of time, of course that is, the mid-point of that straight line—is when this male God's only son, a being half-human and half-divine, appears on the Earth—and on a very specific part of the Earth, one might add—with the purpose in mind of teaching man truth, love, and humble forgiveness, a project not entirely successful, it would seem, if one is to judge by events, today, in *that* part of the world. And the end of that straight line, of course, comes Armageddon, the destruction of the universe by this same male God, the end of the Earth, the end of life, the end of time. I, for one, like to call this great "superstructure" the Book-of-Genesis-to-the-Book-of-Revelation straight line.

The first point to note about this particular mythology, of course, is that there is but one God; that is to say, the dream world it defines is monotheistic in structure, "mono" meaning "one" in ancient Greek, meaning that it is a monotheistic collective subconscious of which we speak here, a monotheistic universe. The second point to note is that this one God is male, and male exclusively. And heterosexual male, one must add here, one with not one conceivable speck of feminine attribute, physical, emotional, biological, or otherwise. The third point to note is that he is perfect, flawless; there is not one thing wrong with him; he knows everything, sees everything, feels everything, can do everything, including stop wars, one would think. The fourth point to note is that time, in this mythology, is of the essence and space, meaning the planet, the universe, our environment, meaning air and water, soil, vegetation, and all that sustains us, is of little to no consequence. And the fifth point is that this time functions according to the principle and structure of one straight line, a line that travels from point A to point B to point C. The sixth point? In the act of creating this universe, there was no sexual act between two partners, no physical pleasure, no extended period of pregnancy, no biological process remotely conceivable; poof, the world just happened, in six short days. And, last, this male God gave us this Earth, and then snatched it away from us—the narrative of eviction from a garden, because of a woman's stupidity, is a narrative that, so far as I know, exists in three mythologies, and three mythologies only—Christian, Judaic, and Islamic—the only three mythologies extant on the

Earth, so far as I know, that, not quite coincidentally, are monotheistic in structure, that have one God only. Space, in other words, was taken from us, and time is our curse.

The second mythology under discussion here, of course, differs quite dramatically on all these points. Greek mythology, first of all, defines a collective subconscious that is polytheistic in structure, "poly" meaning many in ancient Greek. In this universe, that is to say, there is not just one but many gods. And many, many godd*esses*. An epidemic of divine fecundity far too active, and far too exciting, to give fair treatment to, in a talk so very brief as this; suffice it to say that in this dream world, there was a god of the sky, for example, a god the father, if you will, whose name was Zeus (Jupiter in Roman mythology, a mythology which, by the way, came to appropriate this body of narrative round about the middle of the first millennium B.C.). There was a goddess of the Earth, a Mother Earth figure whose name was Hera (Juno in Latin). There was a goddess of love—a goddess of physical, sensual pleasure, that is to say, a goddess of, horrors, sex!—whose name was Aphrodite, from whence, of course, comes the term, in English, for aphrodisiac, among others. There was a goddess of grain whose name was Demeter (Ceres in Latin, from whence, of course, comes the English word for "cereal"). There was even a god of parties, of wild-downtown-Toronto-hotel-room-pagan-type celebrations, whose name, of course, was Dionysus (Bacchus in Latin, from whence, of course, comes the English word bacchanalia). There were messenger gods, gods of the sea, goddesses of the afterlife, a goddess of the home, a goddess of the hunt, gods of this, gods of that, gods of this, gods of that, *ad infinitum*— Apollo, Hestia, Athena, Hermes, Poseidon, Hades, Persephone, the list goes on; in fact, there seems not a single twitch of the human organism *and* of nature for which the Greeks didn't have a god or a goddess, much like, for example, Shinto mythology of Japan that has, to this day, over eight hundred gods *and* goddesses, including gods of trees and of wind and of such celestial bodies as the Sun.

The creation of the Earth, and of the universe, moreover, was made by a patently physical, biological act between an ancient male god, whom few have ever heard of but some accounts say was a wind called Ophion, others say was Boreas (from whence, of course, comes the English word for "boreal," as in "boreal forest")—a wind who wound his immense "physicality" around a female force of energy called Eurynome, which copulative connection gave birth to the universe with its stars and its moons and its planets, including one that eventually came to be known as Earth, the goddess Eurynome, a female herself who eventually came to be known, by the Greeks, as Gaia, precursor to other Mother Earth goddesses through the centuries and eventually to the aforementioned Mother Earth goddess known as Hera. And Mother Earth Hera mated, through no time specified, with Father Sky Zeus and out of *that* union came all the other gods and goddesses, and so it goes. Trees were divinities named Dryads, rivers were goddesses known as Naiads, reeds by the river were gods, sound was a god in the person of a cute little god called, in Greek as in English, Echo. And so it goes, a salient feature to note about these gods and goddesses being that none were perfect; all had the flaws of real-life, four-dimensional, flesh-and-blood human beings. Hera, for example, would traumatize the Earth with her great fits of jealousy whenever she got wind of the fact that her husband, Zeus-in-the-guise-of-swan, had made love to a princess of Sparta named Leda, to name but one Zeus dalliance, which human princess then gave birth to a demi-goddess whom we all know as Helen . . . of Troy. Aphrodite's amorous exploits were legendary. As were Pan's, in the garden of . . . well, more on that shortly.

There was, moreover, no sense of time—or at least no all-pervasive, obsessive sense of it—in this story of creation, or in Greek mythology as a whole. Nature came to fruition—as propelled by these divinities, forces of nature everyone of them—in no particular order; it just flourished, over an unspecified period of time, as one great act of pleasure, one great act of spectacular beauty. (Not, by the way, that pain and suffering didn't exist among the ancient Greeks but . . . more on this in the section on Aboriginal mythology.) Space, in other words, was much more important than was time. Interestingly enough therefore, if this mythology doesn't function according to the rigours of one straight line of time at the beginning, time in the middle, and time at the end, it also does not function quite like a complete circle, more like a circle interrupted and thus, at the very least a curve, a sort of grand semi-circle. And the reason for this interruption of the circle, of course, is because of what happened, historically, in that part of the world, round about the time of the birth of Christ, that point in time where Roman civilization—and thus Roman mythology—had taken over completely from the Greeks and Christian mythology, in its turn, came to supplant Roman mythology. For mythologies, it would seem—as with the gods and goddesses that live therein—have limited life spans, limited periods of usefulness; they are born, they flourish, they fade, they die. Which is where new gods—and goddesses—spring from a battlefield covered, all too often, in blood, ashes, and empty hulks of temples, of churches.

Thus, the most important features to note about this second mythology, for the purposes of this lecture are: A) There is not just one god but many; this is a polytheistic universe, a polytheistic dream world that we speak of. B) God is not exclusively male or exclusively female, but is both at one and the same time. C) None of these gods, or goddesses, is perfect; they all have real emotions, they all have genuine physical sensations, desires, frailties, and such. D) Space is more important than is time. E) Time functions not according to the rigours of one straight line but as a sort of expansive curve, a grand semi-circle, a circle that has been punctured in the middle and then cut in half . . . of which more shortly. F) These were gods of pleasure; they got angry, yes, and they fought here and there but, first and foremost, what they were here for was a good time, a grand celebration of the fact of nature and its miraculous inner workings; the universe and its contents, in other words, were born out of an act of sex, an act of patent biological, and pleasurable, reality. G) As for Paradise or the Garden of Eden, the closest thing the Greeks had to it was Arcadia, a region of Greece still called Arcadia today. There was no eviction; humankind was not kicked out of the garden of joy, that great space of pleasure, the garden of his fleshly desires, by an angry male god; rather was that space a gift from a benevolent—well, mostly benevolent—female god known as Mother Earth, a garden so very beautiful that one god from among the great pantheon of twelve forsook his residence on the airy heights of Mount Olympus to come and live, instead, a life of pleasure—including much sex—right there in the garden; half-goat, half-man in physical shape, an exciting, excitable, perpetually aroused deity, his name was Pan, from whence, of course, comes the English word for "panic," only in this context, the kind of "panic of pleasure" we all feel when sex is on the horizon . . . right there, smack dab in the middle of, precisely, *the garden.*

And the third mythology under discussion here, of course, as I promised, is North American Aboriginal mythology. Accounts vary widely across the continent, as they did in ancient Greece, as they did in the ancient Middle East, but the general consensus—at least in Cree—seems to be that the universe and its contents came into being as the result of the efforts of a female force of energy known as O-ma-ma, a miraculous entity eventually to be known, in the English language, as Mother Earth. Interestingly enough, moreover, in this particular account, there appears to be no overwhelming evidence of masculine involvement in the process of procreation. Hm, turkey basters must have existed back then, one may speculate, the point of the matter being that this girl was end lessly sexual, endlessly sensual, endlessly fertile, a creature of pleasure, a creature of the flesh who gave birth, in no particular order, with no great fixation on the concept of time, to many, many most wondrous and most, most beautiful things . . . including, at the start of her tale, this laughing, hysterically funny, totally outrageous clown called, in English, the Trickster—who, by the way, is half-human and half-god, like all superheroes in practically all mythologies on the planet. Mother Earth then, of course, also gave birth to women. And then men, as an afterthought. And mosquitoes, by the way. And blackflies. And little cells who don't quite always work out in the human bloodstream as cells and cause such illnesses as cancer. But then of course, there were trees, there were flowers, there were lakes, loons, whippoorwills, there was sunset and the wind.

The problem, however, with trying to describe such a concept of divinity in English, one would think, is the same problem one might encounter in attempting to describe Greek divinity, and Greek concepts, in English, which is that it doesn't quite work. There is, for one thing—and most importantly—no concept of gender in the Cree language. In that language, we are all, in a sense, he/shes, trees are he/shes, ocelots are he/shes, budgie-birds in cages are he/shes, even rocks on the beaches of Rio are he/shes. And God—most essentially—is one big fat he/she. Meaning to say that God, even though she may be female in shape biologically in the context of Aboriginal mythology, is both male *and* female simultaneously, emotionally, spiritually, intellectually . . . as are we all, either to a greater or to a lesser extent, depending on who we are, and regardless of whether we are male biologically or female biologically, right? Right.

Second, this god/goddess known, again in English—damn that accursed language—is far from perfect. Yes, she is beautiful, yes, she is grand. And yes, she is generous, she is bountiful, she is kind and ever-loving and supportive and affectionate and all those good things. But she can, like the goddess Hera in Greek mythology when tried to the limit by a masculine side of her that is not quite in working order, she can be one jealous, furiously angry bitch from hell. She kills with earthquakes, she destroys with hurricanes, she destroys with famine and starvation and drought and AIDS, tuberculosis, meningitis, all manner of disorders, physical, emotional, mental, spiritual and otherwise, she tortures with blackflies in July, snowstorms in February, at least in Canada; one really has to be quite careful, but . . . in the end, she is beautiful and kind and, because of it, to be respected, revered, thanked. The point here being that, in Aboriginal mythology, there exists not one God as in Christian mythology, nor many gods, as in Greek mythology, but, rather, the concept of "God in all" or "God in everything"—in Aboriginal mythology, that is to say, we speak not of "monotheism" or of "polytheism" but of "pantheism," the Greek word "pan" meaning all, as in "panorama," or in "pan-American." Meaning that all of nature—from leaves to soil to water to the cat in your living room to the heart inside your body to the woman, or the man, in your life—virtually pulsates with divinity. In the field of cellular biology, they call the notion, I do believe, animism; in mythology *and* theology, we call it pantheism. Same idea, same story.

Next, if time in Greek mythology took second place to space in the great scheme of things, then the distance or gap between that time and that space, in Aboriginal mythology, is of even greater width; in fact, that gap is one huge chasm that is all but unbridgeable, the same case—only in reverse— that exists in the sphere of Christian mythology. That is to say, if time lords it over space in Christian mythology, space lords it over time in Aboriginal mythology.

So that if time, in Christian mythology, is conceived of as one straight line, an arrow that travels with speed accelerating from point A to B to C, and ends there quite abruptly, then time, in Aboriginal mythology, is one vast circle. Or rather *was*, at one point in history, as was the case with Greek mythology before Judaic/Christian mythology came along, in the thousand years between 500 B.C. and 500 A.D., to break it open and, out of it, make a semi-circle, as it were. And within that circle—of Aboriginal mythology—within that womb, to give the notion some visceral perspective, of course, lies the vast expanse of space, the vast expanse of land, the vast expanse of ocean, the vast expanse of air, the vast expanse of sunlight, of lakes—up here in Canada—of lakes unlimited, of forests unlimited, of wildlife unlimited, of a garden of pleasure, a garden of joy unlimited *and* of beauty unlimited and most, most wondrous. And on that circle—of time—moreover, there is no beginning, there is no middle, there is no end. Existence in the universe is merely one endless circle of birth and life and death and re-birth and life and death and re-birth and life and death so that those who lived in times before us—our mothers, our grandmothers, our great-great-grandmothers, those children of ours who have died, those loved ones—they live here with us, still, today, in the very air we breathe, in the shimmer of a leaf on that old oak tree, in that slant of sunlight that falls in through your window and lands on your wrist. They are here. Tears of sorrow are to be shed, yes, but tears of joy as well, tears of rampant celebration.

Last, of course, comes the notion of paradise, of the Garden of Eden. Keeping in mind that there are only three mythologies extant the whole world over at the very heart of which rests the tale of a woman talking to a snake and thus earning all of us eviction from ourselves until the day we die, there is no such myth, no such narrative, in Aboriginal mythology (just as there is none in its Greek counterpart, just as there is none in all other world mythologies, that I know of anyway). According to that narrative, the way that dream world, that collective subconscious, is structured, in other words, we are *still* in that garden. The Sinai Peninsula, after all, may be a parched, treeless desert that has been cursed, and cursed most spectacularly, by an angry male God. And why angry, one may ask? Wouldn't *you* be angry if you hadn't had sex in five thousand years? Which reminds me . . . if he has no wife like Zeus did, or no girlfriend, of which the Trickster had very many, then just how did he get his rocks off . . . keeping in mind that you are looking straight at one of them legendary *retired* altar boys from hell, ouch! And keeping in mind that, at the very least, the Greek God the Father, Zeus—direct precursor to the Roman Jupiter, which name was subsequently shortened to Jove, which name was subsequently

45

appropriated by Judaic and Christian mythology to Jehovah and thence to Yahweh and thus to the deity we know here today as God the Father—keeping in mind that the Greek God the Father, Zeus-in-the-guise-of-eagle made love to a boy named Ganymede, the sun god Apollo had a good friend in a young man named Hyacinth, the pleasure god Pan a good friend in a young man named Narcissus, that is, among his virtual army of Maenads, the point here is that, at the very least, the Greeks were honest about the biological reality both divine *and* human of the singular act of sex and of physical pleasure. Yes, the Sinai Peninsula may be a parched, treeless desert, cursed forever—very obviously—by an angry male god, but Canada, North America, our land, is *not*. North America, quite on the other hand, is the most spectacularly beautiful continent on Earth, as all who have seen it can attest. It is not a curse from an angry male. It is a gift from a benevolent *female* god. That is the difference. And the great Tree of Knowledge, which poor Eve had the bad luck to eat from, because of some overly-masculine narrator, perhaps? Well, in one mythology, we as a species are *not* to partake of such fruit. In the other two, *that's* why it's there; that tree of knowledge is there, right there in the middle of the garden for us to partake of, for us to enjoy, for us to celebrate every day, twice, thrice a day if we have to.

Therefore, ladies and gentlemen, just as Greek mythology came along at one point in the great turning wheel of gods and goddesses through the history of the world as we know it, Christian mythology arrived here on the shores of North America in October of the year 1492. At which point God as man met God as woman—for that's where she'd been kept hidden all this time, as it turns out—and thereby hangs a tale of what are probably the worst cases of rape, wife battery, and attempted wife murder in the history of the world as we know it. At that point in time, in other words, the circle of matriarchy was punctured by the straight line of patriarchy, the circle of the womb, was punctured, most brutally, by the straight line of the phallus. And the bleeding was profuse.

Circles, however, and fortunately, can be repaired. Or an erect phallus can be . . . um . . . doused with ice water? severed completely?—before it's too late. And perhaps, just perhaps what we're looking at today, as we see what's happening in the Middle East—*or* what's about to happen any minute now—perhaps what we're looking at is the death of the male god and the rebirth of the female. We have, after all, very little choice, it seems to me. And, thankfully, as you look out all around you, just from the perspective of sociology alone, we may be seeing just *that*: genders formerly kept silent by the fury—some might say, by the fear—of the one very alone, and very lonely male god taking their lives and the lives of their communities into their own hands, into their own *healing* hands.

Science, after all, in all its brilliance—from quantum physics to cellular biology—has never, so far, yet been able to explain exactly where the impulse of that first cell in the universe came from. And neither has religion, in all its brilliance, in all its incredible complexity, been able to explain, adequately, just where the life force of the common human being originates, where the movement inside that first cell inside the human body comes from. A new language had therefore to be invented—by the visionaries, the priests, the shamans, of our respective societies—to articulate that origin. And that language is *mythology*, the dream world where exist, where thrive men with wings, horses with wings, creatures half-man and half-horse once walked this Earth, beings walk about who are half-man and half-goat just like the god Pan, or who are half-woman half-fish, half-man half-coyote, just like the Native Trickster, or who are half-woman and half-spider, again like the Native Trickster, snakes talk to women (but not to men), women give birth without having had sex, dead men rise from the grave. And men—and women, too—are human and divine at one and the same time.

Mythology, the exact halfway point between truth and fiction, mythology, the exact halfway point between science and religion, that most elaborate of all fictions. Truth, mythology, fiction.

Tomson Highway

Science, mythology, religion, the ultimate, the original circle. And thereby hangs an enormous, and very long, story . . . of which more later.

Thank you.